ASPATORE
BOOKS

C-LEVEL BUSINESS INTELLIGENCE · C-LEVEL BUSINESS INTELLIGENCE · C-LEVEL BUSINESS INTELLIGENCE ·

www.Aspatore.com

Aspatore Books is the largest and most exclusive publisher of C-Level executives (CEO, CFO, CTO, CMO, Partner) from the world's most respected companies and law firms. Aspatore annually publishes a select group of C-Level executives from the Global 1,000, top 250 law firms (Partners & Chairs), and other leading companies of all sizes. C-Level Business Intelligence™, as conceptualized and developed by Aspatore Books, provides professionals of all levels with proven business intelligence from industry insiders – direct and unfiltered insight from those who know it best – as opposed to third-party accounts offered by unknown authors and analysts. Aspatore Books is committed to publishing an innovative line of business and legal books, those which lay forth principles and offer insights that when employed, can have a direct financial impact on the reader's business objectives, whatever they may be. In essence, Aspatore publishes critical tools – need-to-read as opposed to nice-to-read books – for all business professionals.

Inside the Minds

The critically acclaimed *Inside the Minds* series provides readers of all levels with proven business intelligence from C-Level executives (CEO, CFO, CTO, CMO, Partner) from the world's most respected companies. Each chapter is comparable to a white paper or essay and is a future-oriented look at where an industry/profession/topic is heading and the most important issues for future success. Each author has been carefully chosen through an exhaustive selection process by the *Inside the Minds* editorial board to write a chapter for this book. *Inside the Minds* was conceived in order to give readers actual insights into the leading minds of business executives worldwide. Because so few books or other publications are actually written by executives in industry, *Inside the Minds* presents an unprecedented look at various industries and professions never before available.

Other Books for Investment Banking Professionals

INSIDE THE MINDS:
Leading
Investment Bankers
The Art & Science of Investment Banking

Published by Aspatore Books, Inc.
For corrections, company/title updates, comments or any other inquiries please email info@aspatore.com.

First Printing, 2002
10 9 8 7 6 5 4 3 2 1

ISBN 1-58762-061-8

Library of Congress Card Number: 2002092000

Edited by Jo Alice Hughes, Proofread by Ginger Conlon, Cover design by Kara Yates & Ian Mazie

Material in this book is for educational purposes only. This book is sold with the understanding that neither any of the authors or the publisher is engaged in rendering legal, accounting, investment, or any other professional service.

This book is printed on acid free paper.

A special thanks to all the individuals that made this book possible.

Special thanks to: Kirsten Catanzano, Melissa Conradi, Molly Logan, Justin Hallberg

Inside the Minds:
Leading Investment Bankers
The Art & Science of Investment Banking

Contents

A MULTIDISCIPLINARY APPROACH: CRUCIAL TO M&A SUCCESS

DANIEL H. BAYLY

Merrill Lynch & Co., Inc.

Chairman of Global Investment Banking

Integrity and Client Focus

The primary objective of every investment banker must be providing excellent advice and guidance that clients can trust, whether they are considering a major merger, an acquisition, or a critical financing. Bankers must ensure that every client receives a carefully constructed, thoughtful plan that has considered all alternatives and their potential ramifications. Every aspect of each option must be examined with the view to assisting the company in its selection of the alternative that will create the most shareholder value within a tolerable risk parameter.

The team that constructs this plan should draw upon years of experience and specialization in each banker's designated discipline. Communication and coordination between the individual groups that contribute value must be seamless. The client's best interest is the foremost objective of this process. Bankers must be trained to work as a team toward this objective, a team that does not try to create unanimity, but actually tries to create the solution that produces the most shareholder value.

The key to all this is "focused teamwork." One banker, a relationship manager, must orchestrate the process and ensure that all of a firm's capabilities and resources are focused on the client's opportunities and challenges. However, the strength and power of the advice is heavily based on the collective capabilities of the team members. It is this dedication and experience, coupled with the willingness of each team member to work seamlessly with the other members of the team – without regard for any personal credit or agenda – that creates tremendous value for the client. The Merrill Lynch bankers are trained to have great respect for their colleagues and fellow employees who are both senior and junior to them. This culture of respect permeates the organization. Men and women from very different backgrounds come together to create value for clients. As a global organization dedicated to clients around the world, this diversity is our strength.

For clients in general, and for the investment banking industry in particular, the past decade has yielded remarkable change – and remarkable opportunity. Historically, when industry changes have been rapid, the opportunities have been more dramatic. Recently, there have been four global trends that have accelerated this theory.

Globalization: As corporations seek worldwide growth opportunities, they build and acquire assets in many new strategic locations. This activity creates a large amount of investment banking business, as these investments typically require substantial new capital.

The outbreak of capitalism: The trend toward free, democratic societies and nations releasing the creative and entrepreneurial spirit of their people provides huge growth opportunities for our clients and the investment banking community in general.

Technology: The rapid advancement of global technology and communications has dramatically improved the ability of governments and corporations to operate efficiently and produce much more value for their stakeholders. More efficient organizations rapidly free up new capital, further accelerate change, and create new business opportunities.

Elimination of trade barriers: The rise of the European market, NAFTA, and other free trading zones are very positive global trends that encourage the flow of capital and new investments across borders previously characterized by governmental economic constraints.

All of these global trends provide opportunities for clients and, as a result, for the investment banking industry. Before these developments, the investment banking business appeared relatively mature and largely constrained by domestic boundaries and local markets. These trends have transformed the business into a global growth opportunity. This is one primary reason traditional commercial banks see greater opportunity in the investment banking business and are trying to find entry by acquiring or developing new investment banking products and services. As these four trends have accelerated global change, the past decade has seen the rise of the investment banking firms that have the global scope, full-service capabilities, and the experience to service clients in these demanding, complex, and rapidly changing markets.

As clients have become more global, requiring increasingly sophisticated services, the investment banking community has responded creatively to their needs. As a result, the capital markets themselves have become much more liquid and global. Facilitated by the investment banks creating new markets in a variety of debt, equity, and derivative securities, and acting as both principal and agent, corporations are able to access new sources of capital to grow and expand their businesses. Liquid currency markets, again facilitated by both the investment banks and commercial banks as intermediaries, provide ready conversion to local currencies in any fully developed market.

As corporations and markets become more global, faster, and much more complex, the risk to clients expands exponentially. Managing this risk and all the relevant components is always a critical aspect of any investment banking assignment. Clients see tremendous global opportunity, but achieving their goals depends largely on managing the incumbent risk. This may be a risk in connection with a client's investment opportunities for more revenue growth. It may be the risk of a large acquisition or divestiture; balance-sheet risk; risk associated with an equity, equity-linked, or straight debt financing; or perhaps a currency or interest rate swap. Assisting the client in managing this risk and balancing it with a carefully orchestrated process of raising capital, or advising on a major M&A transaction, is the principle challenge for our investment bankers. Every transaction executed for clients must be designed to manage this risk while simultaneously increasing shareholder value. Those objectives, in all cases, are the basis for our advice.

The Importance of Relationship Management

To best assist the company in achieving these objectives, bankers are becoming increasingly very specialized. We have experts in each industry and product discipline who are very experienced in providing the most comprehensive advice to our clients. Our bankers must thoroughly understand all the positives and potential negatives associated with a particular course of action. The specialists are linked by the relationship manager, who has overall client focus and responsibility, and who must seamlessly orchestrate the team members to assist the client in achieving the most favorable outcome. These specialists are corporate finance professionals who are experts in designing financial solutions to fit a particular client's requirements; equity, equity-linked, or debt capital market specialists; or industry specialists. Each of these professionals has an in-depth understanding of the dynamics of a particular industry, including the issues that drive value and present challenges. Like corporate finance professionals or capital market specialists, industry specialists work globally and have a comprehensive view of customers, competitors, and suppliers, and they can provide advice to clients based on broad experience and in-depth knowledge.

This approach is critical in assessing the strengths and weaknesses of a client's current competitive positions and the feasibility of the client's objectives and goals within the context of an acceptable risk profile. Within this framework, if financing is required, we first undertake a detailed analysis of the client's financial position. This involves full familiarization with the client's income statement, balance sheet, cash flow capabilities, and issues such as the rating agencies' view of the company and the company's relative market position. Earnings, cash flow, and balance-sheet projections under different sets of assumptions will be done to help determine the best course of action and whether additional financing is actually necessary. Only after this review is completed can we recommend a security that best meets the needs of the client.

When Banco do Brasil wanted to raise $300 million, we structured the first ever financial future flow securitization out of Brazil, which opened a more than $2 billion market for future structured issuance by Brazilian banks. This transaction securitized workers' remittances for Banco do Brasil, the largest financial institution in the country. Brazilian workers who live in Japan send, on a regular basis, part of their salary to relatives in Brazil. Flows are processed via Banco do Brasil, which is the leader in the remittance market in Japan. This was a very innovative way to reduce the cost of funding for Brazilian banks. It was the highest rated transaction ever executed by a Brazilian entity – priced more than 400 basis points inside Brazil's benchmark five-year bond. This is an excellent example, in the global marketplace, of an investment banking team, comprising the critical product and country specialists, working together to design a transaction tailored to a client's particular need.

Revolutionary Evolution

This corporate finance creativity and comprehensive understanding of a client's situation is required in most transactions and is the basis for most of the "value added" service an investment bank provides. Frequently, the client's solution starts with a new idea created by our corporate finance group. The original concept may have been improved over time, evolving with a succession of innovations that enhance the original. The genesis of this evolutionary process is almost always a client who has a particular problem or requirement. By understanding a particular client's problems, we devise a new solution for that situation. Often, other clients have the same requirements and can use a similar or slightly altered version of the original idea.

An excellent example of an original idea that, with added features and innovations over a period of years, has revolutionized a portion of the capital markets is Merrill Lynch's 1985 invention of Liquid Yield Option Notes (LYONS). LYONS is a zero coupon financing that is convertible into the issuer's common stock at increasing premiums. Even though the issuer pays no interest, he takes tax deductions at the stated coupon rate. There is no debate over the tax treatment, however, because the purchaser of the instrument agrees to pay taxes, even though he receives no interest payments. This concept was extremely innovative, and for a long time Merrill Lynch was the only firm to execute LYONS transactions. Over the past few years we have dramatically enhanced the product with features such as contingent conversion and contingent payment that create even more value for the issuer. Through these types of new capital markets products, each designed to fit a particular client need, the convertible or equity-linked market has been expanded and transformed. Today the equity-linked market actually rivals the pure equity market in terms of absolute size. In the first six months of 2002 total issuance in the U.S. of straight equity has been about $45 billion, and equity-linked issuance has been about $36 billion. This is an enormous change, and this financing vehicle has provided value to hundreds of issuing clients, as other investment banks have now embraced the structure for the benefit of their own clients.

The largest convertible bond transaction in the first half of 2002 was the $3.75 billion Series A&B contingently convertible senior debentures offering for General Motors. Both convertible bonds had 30-year maturities; however, Series A had a "put" in year 5, and Series B had a put in year 12. This structure was a highly efficient way for General Motors to raise a substantial amount of additional capital. This transaction occurred only after an exhaustive analysis of all types of equity and equity-linked structures by both the General Motors treasury team and our corporate finance group and equity capital markets professionals.

Finessing Financing and the M&A Process

Although each transaction necessitates a very thorough analysis and review of alternatives, all successful transactions are part art and part science. In every deal the judgment of the bankers is absolutely critical. This is another reason an interdisciplinary team must be available and must be able to communicate and cooperate seamlessly, keeping the best interest of the client as their focus and primary objective. Nowhere is this more important than in the mergers and acquisitions (M&A) business – which is probably the most sensitive type of transaction in terms of creating or destroying value. In a financing such as those discussed above, a mistake in timing, pricing, or structuring can cost a client millions of dollars. But in M&A, depending on the relative size of the transaction, the viability of the enterprise can hang in the balance.

We have highly capable, experienced M&A professionals who are deeply knowledgeable about various technical strategies and about their particular industry. These professionals work on behalf of many clients seeking to enhance their business through a strategic transaction.

The process may begin with our M&A professionals working with a particular client over a long period to evaluate their competitive position. We try to develop a clear view of our client's ability to build and sustain a competitive advantage with its current business and product portfolio. In many cases our clients have already initiated and completed a value-based, analytical approach using EVA (economic value added) or similar methodology, and our investment bankers can benefit from this analysis. EVA is designed to distinguish between divisions and products consistently able to earn returns in excess of their cost of capital and contribute to the growth of the entire enterprise.

After the analysis and review are complete, which can require months of work, and when the client concludes they can improve their competitive position or create value by restructuring, we will begin a comprehensive review of the strategic options. Acquisitions of competitors, full integration strategies, divestitures, joint ventures, spin-offs, IPOs, stock repurchases, and asset swaps are all examined in careful detail. If ideal strategic partners can be narrowed down or specifically identified, the analysis begins to focus on valuation, structure, tactics, and other execution issues. Integral to this phase of the process is a complete financial review. Conclusions are partially based on the company's projections of combined revenues, earnings, cash flow, margin analysis, return on invested capital, and balance-sheet ramifications, as well as an accretion/dilution analysis under different business scenarios.

A more comprehensive valuation analysis will often be conducted using a variety of valuation methodologies. Typical valuation techniques include discounted cash flow analysis (with various discount rates), public comparables analysis, acquisition comparables analysis, and an LBO (leveraged buy-out) analysis, as well as pro forma analysis for the most likely strategic buyers (and calculating their "ability to pay"). We will also sometimes examine where the bulk of the shareholder base accumulated their share position and conduct a broad analysis of takeover premiums, given the overall levels of the stock markets.

In a buy-side assignment all of this is factored into an equation that includes a judgment of whether other companies could bid or challenge the potential transaction. If intense competition for the target is expected, it may change the investment banker's opinion concerning the premium that may ultimately be necessary. Significant time is also spent structuring deal-protection mechanisms, such as no-shop clauses, break-up fees, and the right to match any competing proposal. A complete regulatory assessment from all of the participants advising the company *(e.g.,* the client's lawyers and finance team, outside lawyers, public relations firms, and investment bankers) must be made especially to look at the combination from an antitrust standpoint. A judgment must determine whether the transaction could be challenged from an antitrust perspective and what remedies would be required.

There also needs to be a thorough review of the target's and the client's shareholder profiles. M&A bankers will consider whether a particular tax or structural solution can facilitate a transaction between buyer and seller by removing an otherwise addressable impediment. In conjunction with this, a careful assessment must be made of the client's potential vulnerability to takeover. The team must also review the client's defensive preparedness to ensure maximum protection. Lack of careful preparation in this regard can trigger an unwanted series of developments, making the company more vulnerable to a hostile bid, bear hug, or other coercive activity and potentially lead to a change in control.

Other critical issues when considering a major acquisition are the issues of leadership. Many M&A transactions are not completed because of "social issues," such as management roles, location of headquarters, board composition, and combined company name. The leadership of the new company in terms of who is the new CEO, and whom his executive committee will comprise, is always very delicate, and advisors frequently play an important role in negotiating the outcome. If the two organizations are substantially different in size, the issue of the CEO position is usually clear, and the transaction is deemed more a takeover than a "merger of equals." When the market capitalizations are relatively close, however, this can be a very difficult issue and can terminate combination discussions that otherwise have compelling strategic logic. Frequently, the issue gets decided on the basis of the relative success of the two enterprises, which business has a stronger outlook, and many other considerations, including the experience, stature, and age of the two CEOs, and their ability and prior experience in integrating businesses.

A Tale of Two Transactions

Perhaps the most notable strategic initiative that has had a negative impact on shareholder value in 2002 was not a business combination, but the restructuring of Tyco International, a diversified manufacturing and service company. Tyco CEO Dennis Kozlowski, who resigned in June 2002, had originally designed a well-received but very aggressive business model over the past 10 years. The model was partially constructed around an acquisition program that accumulated businesses very rapidly in an attempt to build critical mass in four or five core business groups. In accounting for many of these transactions, Tyco was able to significantly supplement organic EPS (earnings per share) growth. In other words, almost all Tyco's deals were accretive to EPS, which is a practice widely used by almost every major corporation doing acquisitions. In this case, however, there were so many transactions that the accounting became very complex and subsequently drew a great deal of scrutiny from many analysts and investors. In doing the deals, the company used both cash and equity as media of exchange, and was careful to maintain a strong balance sheet, not become excessively leveraged, and not lose Tyco's investment grade credit rating. The model was also heavily dependent on aggressive cost cutting, a decentralized operating structure, and a generous incentive system for high-level performers. This business model attracted institutional investors who were seeking rapidly growing companies, and Tyco was awarded a premium valuation. But the key question was whether Tyco could keep doing larger and larger accretive acquisitions to sustain the very rapid growth of EPS that Wall Street investors now expected.

At some point, Kozlowski and his advisors decided that Tyco could best create additional shareholder value by restructuring the company. On January 22, Tyco announced its intention to split the company into four independent, publicly traded companies – security and electronics, healthcare, fire protection/ flow control, and CIT (finance). Under the terms of the plan, Tyco would sell its plastics business and IPO or spin off the healthcare, fire protection/flow control, and CIT businesses. Tyco's equity market capitalization at the time of the announcement was approximately $93 billion. By late April the equity market capitalization of Tyco had fallen to approximately $43 billion. Shareholders had lost about $50 billion in three months. At this point, Tyco changed direction and decided to cancel the split-up. The stock then continued to fall as many accounting questions persisted and Kozlowski resigned.

The science of evaluating the breakup of Tyco was complex, but the process was relatively straightforward for an investment banker. While there are many complicated reasons this strategic initiative failed, one important oversight was that institutional shareholders heavily supported Kozlowski's original business model. The breakup envisioned an entirely different business model built around the "pure play" of each individual division operating within its own distinct industry. In the new plan these divisions would not be part of a rapidly growing, acquisition-oriented business in connection with Tyco's acquisition program led by Kozlowski, who had proved he could make his particular model work. Nearly every shareholder had bought stock in one business concept and strategy, and now every shareholder would own four entirely new and unproven business models where the business strategies would have a new, untested leader.

Consequently, most major shareholders (Tyco had two billion shares outstanding) probably wanted to restructure their portfolios – at the same time. This may have created significant selling pressure on Tyco's stock. It simply demonstrates that all potential ramifications, including reactions of the stock market and the shareholder base, must be very carefully considered. Ultimately, the value of each individual Tyco business unit might conform to the science of the original analysis, but many shareholders would have traded out of their original position. Many other critical factors that subsequently surfaced were also involved in the market's reaction and the stock's decline, including general concerns surrounding the extremely difficult situation at Enron, the accounting questions, and Kozlowski's resignation.

A more successful strategic transaction was Comcast's bid to acquire ATT Broadband out of ATT for approximately $72 billion. This initiative, launched by Comcast, caused ATT to reconsider its plan to IPO the cable business, which was ultimately put up for auction – and Comcast was the successful bidder. Comcast identified an opportunity that made good strategic sense and, in conjunction with its advisors (Merrill Lynch being one), devised a plan to pursue its objective. They recognized that ATT shareholder value would be better served by selling the business than by the planned IPO. By publicly expressing their interest, they essentially "bear-hugged" the opportunity and changed the strategic plan of ATT through both compelling economic logic and the weight of shareholder opinion. They also gained the initial momentum to ultimately prevail. At the direction of Comcast, an entire team of investment banking specialists helped design this strategy, including M&A professionals, equity and debt capital markets specialists, and industry specialists. This is an excellent example of the corporate client directing an investment banking team that used a multidisciplinary approach, which helped identify a more successful path to create value for shareholders.

As the global trends mentioned earlier continue and gain momentum, clients will be increasingly dependent on a seamless multidisciplinary approach, which is tightly focused on the client's best interest and delivered with absolute integrity. However, in a faster, more complex global marketplace, clients are inherently assuming more risk. They are venturing into new geographic regions and countries with different cultures, business practices, regulatory systems, and different accounting and tax laws.

Many industries are currently consolidating on a global scale, and all these issues must be carefully addressed before proceeding with any individual transaction. The role of the client's investment banker is obviously more complex than ever, and the investment banker's global scope and full-service capabilities are more critical than ever.

In this new world the CEO is also under much more pressure. There was always tremendous pressure from institutional investors demanding ever-improving results on a quarterly basis. But now the level of scrutiny of a company's financial results has never been higher. As a result of all these factors and the increased pressure, the tenure of CEOs has never been lower. The average tenure of a CEO is now about four years, as opposed to six or seven years as recently as 10 years ago. Despite this highly pressured environment, part of the responsibility of the investment banker (and part of the art of the profession) is to encourage clients to adopt a longer-term, more strategic perspective. Companies must not be pressured into immediate actions designed to boost EPS or the stock price over the short term. Successful companies are built over a period of years. This requires thoughtful, long-range planning, not sporadic actions designed to temporarily appease demanding stockholders seeking immediate returns.

In consolidating industries, the organizations that emerge the strongest are those that are building strategically, in a series of transactions executed over time. Each deal must be integrated and digested before moving to the next opportunity. It also helps tremendously if the CEO and his investment banker have worked together to analyze the trends far in advance and are prepared to move quickly when necessary. Frequently, the organizations that are well-prepared and are able to move earlier than their competitors are the winners. This "early mover" advantage can be critical as these companies move closer to executing the next critical phase of their plan. At the same time, competitors are playing "catch up," and their strategic options have suddenly been narrowed. Being prepared far in advance and deciding when to initiate a transaction tends to be very judgmental and is often more critical than the more scientific dilution/accretion analysis. Consequently, in this highly intense, global, complex environment – where many industries are experiencing rapid consolidation – excellent preparation and a closely knit working team are often the deciding factors between success and failure.

Priorities: People and Principles

The opportunities to serve clients in this new environment are growing rapidly, and as a result, there has also been a proliferation of investment banking firms over the course of the past few years. This has created the unfortunate circumstance that as the demands on the investment banking firms have grown with the growth of the global economy, more firms with much less experience also offer those services. Although consolidation in the financial services industry may continue over the next few years (as it will in many industries), I believe that the differentiating factors among industry leaders for investment banking services will continue to be integrity, client focus, and specialized professionals who are experienced and well coordinated.

People and a dedication to the principles of hard work and integrity are the foundation of excellence, and they always will be the first objective and primary focus of our investment banking effort. We obviously spend a tremendous amount of time on recruiting and identifying the right people. These individuals constitute the future of our firm in particular and the financial services industry in general. Once we have identified the best, highest quality, and brightest people possible, we concentrate on training. An enormous amount of time and expense is invested in these young people, and all senior managers are required to participate in the training process. *Process* is the proper term because our training, while very intense and concentrated at the beginning of a person's career, continues at regular intervals throughout his or her entire career. This continuing education and training are essential to ensure we develop the most professional, highest quality team of investment bankers.

Furthermore, the initial training and guidance individuals receive at the beginning of their careers are critical to their long-term development. This initial training forms the foundation for their professional behavior and for future learning, and consequently, we take new employees' introduction to the firm particularly seriously. As our business grew rapidly, we also hired excellent professionals laterally at different levels of seniority. These individuals receive intensive training and guidance when they join the firm and throughout their careers, as well.

The five Merrill Lynch principles of client focus, respect for the individual, teamwork, responsible citizenship, and integrity are repeatedly stressed. Frequent contact and association with senior professionals who reinforce these principles are absolutely critical as our new colleagues begin to understand and appreciate the strength and culture of the firm.

Merrill Lynch has historically had an outstanding training program, and I believe we are training the next generation of leaders on Wall Street. Many of these employees will stay at Merrill Lynch for many, many years, but others will find new opportunities at other financial institutions. For this reason, Merrill Lynch is training personnel who will, in the future, lead numerous different types of financial services organizations. Scores of current leaders within Wall Street firms started their careers at Merrill Lynch.

Over the years I have spoken to many incoming classes of new associates and analysts. These individuals are typically just graduating from a prominent business school, college, or university. They are usually a very diverse group, coming from different countries, cultures, and personal backgrounds. In addition to providing a detailed review of our investment banking effort and discussing the Merrill Lynch principles, I stress several things:

❑ *View issues from the client's perspective.* Put yourself in the shoes of the CEO and begin to make judgments from this vantage point.

❑ *Take a long-term perspective.* Do not be overly influenced by getting a transaction finished. Think about the long-term ramifications and how a particular deal fits a client's long-term needs.

❏ *Communicate globally.* This skill is critical. Bankers who communicate more actively with their team members tend to produce better client solutions.

❏ *Be proactive.* Initiating ideas, speaking up, and acting immediately on client requests or client problems build momentum and produce creative energy.

❏ *Prioritize your time.* There are tremendous demands on these young people. They must prioritize the most important issues, ask and clearly understand why they are being requested to perform a particular task – and act on the critical objectives first.

❏ *Think first about your clients and colleagues.* This is an excellent policy, and it creates a very powerful impression in the minds of your clients and colleagues who immediately recognize, and tremendously respect, this type of behavior.

❏ *Think strategically.* Usually, a client's objective is to become number one in terms of global market share and quality of performance. This typically takes place over a period of time through a series of thoughtful strategic moves – not in one big transforming transaction.

❏ *Relax and have fun.* Despite the tension and pressure of the business, this is a critical skill – it is frequently the best response to that pressure – to relax and keep things in perspective. Developing this skill helps personal well-being, and it's actually necessary to improve performance.

I give these recommendations at each meeting with incoming classes, and I try to reinforce them at every opportunity. I hope this advice is helpful, but the five Merrill Lynch principles, our training, and our culture are the foundation of our success.

Daniel H. Bayly is chairman of Global Investment Banking and a member of the Executive Management Committee and the Office of the Chairman of Merrill Lynch & Co., Inc. The Investment Banking group provides strategic advisory and financing services to corporations, institutions, and governments on a global basis.

Mr. Bayly, 54, was previously senior vice president and served as head or co-head of the Investment Banking division between 1995 and 2001. Before that, Mr. Bayly held a number of positions in investment banking, including head of Merrill Lynch's North American industrial investment banking business and group head of U.S. Corporate Banking.

WINNING BUSINESS

RICHARD BYRNE

Deutsche Bank

Head of Debt Products and Financial Sponsors

Hub and Spokes: A Model for Success

Investment banking is a relatively simple business. Investment banks derive most of their revenues from advising and financing their clients. Their organizations are structured around these activities. In broad terms, there are two types of investment bankers – relationship bankers and product specialists – and both are an integral part of servicing a client. Investment banking is also a team sport, not a one-on-one proposition, and working together is crucial for success. The two types of bankers form a cohesive unit that matches sophisticated financial advice to the needs of clients and draws on the strength of the investment bank and its resources to complete the job.

Though their roles are different, relationship bankers and product specialists are interdependent. Product specialists have a narrow, highly specialized area of financial expertise and a tremendous amount of experience executing deals in their markets. Relationship bankers have a deep and involved understanding of their clients and broad knowledge of the financial products that are available.

They become a bridge between the client and the investment bank, ensuring that the client receives the attention they need from the appropriate specialists, while also serving as the product group's "eyes and ears" among clients.

An effective way for these two types of bankers to interrelate and best serve the client is through a "hub-and-spokes model," with the relationship banker serving as the central point of contact between the client and the bank. The spokes represent the product specialists and other specialized resources of the firm, such as equity and debt capital markets, mergers and acquisitions, lending, research, and senior management, which are all part of the client team and are all called upon when appropriate. The relationship banker is the point-person for the client, which includes CEOs, CFOs, and other decision-makers, but they act as a hub, not a gatekeeper, coordinating all of the activity. Everyone plays a role that fits into the model. While a healthy tension is likely to exist, firms that can successfully integrate all these points of contact and harness the flow of information will dominate the battle for market share.

Prioritizing to Maximize Revenue

You cannot be all things to all people, so one of the most critical first steps in investment banking is identifying the clients and business lines on which to focus. You must use a methodical process to prioritize clients based on the amount of potential business you can expect them to generate. The top prospects should occupy the vast majority of an investment banking team's time.

Unfortunately, prioritization is very difficult. Target clients are not necessarily firms that have produced the largest historical revenues. You need to be able to foresee market developments and make judgments accordingly. As Wayne Gretzky once said, Don't skate to where the puck is, but to where it is going.

The prioritization process is started by gathering all internal experts on a given sector from across a firm. Using input from the entire team, the competitive landscape is mapped out, and key trends that will have an impact on the industry are identified. Based on these predictions, it can be determined which investment banking services will be needed to best respond to those trends. With all this in mind, each client should be examined carefully to estimate the volume of business they can potentially transact. Finally, the competitive landscape must also be taken into account in determining whether your firm has a legitimate chance of capturing that revenue.

For example, after the merger of Deutsche Bank and Bankers' Trust, we set out to prioritize the business opportunities in the gaming sector. While gaming represented a relatively new business for our bank, several people, including myself, had extensive experience with many of these companies. We assembled a team that included specialists in debt, M&A, equity, research, loans, and other product areas, as well as relationship bankers. As a group, we identified a number of trends we believed would dominate the industry in the short- to medium-term.

After extensive networking and immersing ourselves in data from diverse sources, we concluded the gaming sector was beginning to mature, with fewer new gaming jurisdictions opening and overall growth beginning to slow. As a result, equity valuations were low; larger players were seeking to expand into new markets; and smaller firms were continuing to struggle. Based on these factors, along with a low interest-rate environment and improving credit profiles, we agreed that M&As and debt refinancings would drive gaming deal-flow.

We then analyzed the market to determine which companies were best positioned to take advantage of those trends and would need investment banking services. By combing through detailed financial analyses, we discovered which firms could best capitalize on attractive rates or a different capital structure. By analyzing business plans and competitive positions, we identified potential acquirers and targets. On top of this we overlaid our knowledge of the players and their personalities, as well as our sense as to the competitive landscape. Finally, we had to label as low priority any names we believed were unlikely, for a variety of reasons, to become revenue-generating clients.

The product of our analysis was a three-tiered list. We estimated that the first tier of clients, which were generally the largest firms that should generate the most fees, would occupy at least 75 percent of our time. The second tier was still expected to produce substantial fees, though with less certainty or regularity, and would take about 20 percent. Finally, we decided it was important to cover the rest of the firms because they still played a role in the market and could become larger clients later; however, those firms would require only 5 percent or less of our time.

To maximize revenues, it's important to stay disciplined. But it is also necessary to be adaptable. After we established our list of clients and determined which tier each one belonged in, we regularly modified the list whenever we anticipated changes in the market or at individual firms that could alter the deal landscape. That way we were always directing our resources to where they would maximize returns. Finally, we set a goal for ourselves that we would strive to anticipate *all* new business opportunities, pick our battles and win, and *never* learn about a deal for the first time in the newspaper.

For individuals, another important aspect of prioritizing is eliminating unproductive activities and thought. One constant aspect of investment banking organizations is change. It is easy for individuals to become distracted by organizational flux. I always advise young bankers to put their heads down and focus on their jobs and their clients and set clear and measurable goals. Most organizations are meritocracies, and people who follow this advice will be successful. Over time, a good investment bank will reward superior performance. If you are adding value and revenues, you will be recognized.

Four Pillars of Success

Once you have set up a team and prioritized your clients, there are four building blocks that are crucial for success in investment banking. Relationships are the bedrock upon which deals are built; ideas are the product an investment banker creates; and the ability to deliver your firm's resources enables you to carry out your ideas and maintain your relationships. Last, you must be able to ask for and get the mandate.

Relationships

Good investment bankers are extensions of their clients, a second brain dedicated to ensuring those clients have every advantage and seize every available opportunity, especially in the financial markets. CEOs, CFOs, treasurers, and other senior executives are appropriately focused on their firm and its competitive and operating environment. Successful bankers work to understand that environment almost as well as their clients, and then apply their specialized knowledge of the capital markets and the related accounting, tax, and regulatory provisions, so their clients can focus on their core businesses. Good bankers offer superior insight based on their continuous networking with other industry participants. Ultimately, a banker's job is to help their clients make money. It's a true partnership.

It is often said that a good relationship banker is one with a low golf handicap, access to great tickets, and a flair for selecting great wines, and there's a grain of truth to that. Clients don't stop thinking about work when they leave the office, and to truly understand their motivations, relationships need to extend past the traditional workday. A good banker needs to know his clients' secretaries, spouses, and favorite restaurants. Their families socialize when appropriate, and they should occasionally be prepared to interrupt their own family plans when a client needs to talk. Good bankers talk with their clients on weekends, and the clients know they can call in the middle of the night to discuss an idea. In short, the client becomes part of their life.

All of these things combine to create a bond of trust between a banker and his clients. A good banker becomes a confidante, advisor, and friend. He should know and understand his client's goals and aspirations and offer high-quality, unbiased advice. Most important, he has access. And when you have access to a CEO, it opens the door to the rest of the chain-of-command.

We focus on establishing a "strategic dialogue" with our clients, probing into what they are thinking and what is important to them, and using our team to formulate innovative ideas that engage the client's thought process to generate more dialogue. Establishing this kind of relationship leads to access: The client will tend to choose you because you have more insight, superior perspective, and, above all else, their confidence.

In one instance I was scheduled to fly with the CEO of a major firm from New York to the Southeast to visit a new project they were working on. The client's CFO and other senior executives were scheduled to pick us up on their corporate jet, but they were rerouted because of an approaching storm. The CEO and I took a commercial flight, which subsequently became stranded in a remote airport when the storm shifted course. During the five-hour delay, the CEO and I spent quality time together. He spoke at length about his plans, goals, and ambitions, and after listening I was able to sketch out a financing plan, literally on the back of an envelope, that would help fulfill those goals. When we finally rejoined the rest of the group, it was agreed to put the plan into action.

Ideas

Executives know their own companies well, but they will always have time for bankers who can help them make money. If you discover an innovation in a financial market or a complex financial structure, or if you're the first to identify an opportunity for your clients, you will win business. Even when your clients are unable to adopt or execute your ideas, they often will reward you with a role in another deal to recognize your efforts. It's part of the partnership that develops between the banker and the client.

There is no monopoly on good ideas. Investment banking is an intensely competitive industry, so you have to be smarter and faster than the next guy. Clients expect their bankers not only to be well-versed in the latest innovations and deals, but also to provide advice on how those things affect their business and market. Investment banking teams are an extremely powerful way to bring resources and expertise to the client. Good bankers can adapt ideas from other products and markets to fit the needs of their clients, as well as to identify totally new ideas and opportunities. They also should be ideally situated within their sector to identify opportunities between clients and make introductions that can lead to mergers, divestitures, and joint ventures.

To be an expert at both your own industry and your clients' requires a massive investment of time and hard work, and the process never ends. In addition to understanding all the pieces of the financial world, you must constantly study the latest deals, regulations, market trends, and new ideas, so you can help your clients stay ahead of the game.

Experience is an important asset. All deals have similarities, and by participating in a wide variety of transactions, you learn how to overcome obstacles that will no doubt surface in other deals. You learn techniques and skills you can apply to different types of problems in different types of deals. It's also important to maintain open lines of communication with your colleagues and specialists within your firm, as good ideas often can be adapted from one product, sector, or region to another.

Many investment banks even have a special group of people whose sole job is to generate ideas. They constantly monitor the financial, regulatory, and accounting fields to identify trends and developments that will affect our clients, and they work closely with bankers to turn those ideas into deals. By focusing solely on ideas, they can generate some very creative transactions. These bankers should be integrated into the banking team.

In addition to drawing on your experience and that of your colleagues, it is important to be well-read. Smart bankers go beyond the mainstream financial press to keep their edge and take advantage of the newsletters and magazines that cover specialized areas of finance, such as high-yield bonds or syndicated bank loans or derivatives. They also read the specialty publications that cover their clients' industries, as well as research reports both from inside the firm and from third parties, such as the ratings agencies and consulting firms. Most important, they can extract pertinent ideas from the clutter of information.

Knowledge is power. It is therefore also critical for firms to invest in continuing education and for bankers to take advantage of it. Wall Street's "apprenticeship" involves training associates by allowing them to participate in deals and gain increasing levels of responsibility. This helps provide them with the experience they will draw on later in their careers.

Delivering

Whether you work in an investment banking boutique or a full-service institution, clients will do business with you if you add value. Many small clients continue to consolidate their investment banking activities to a few core firms that offer a full suite of products, services, and expertise. Also, as capital becomes increasingly scarce, clients place a growing priority on firms that can provide it. Clients expect their banks to be a player in all of the major products and to have outstanding research. All of these things are considered the price of admission for the major investment banks. More than ever, bankers need a platform behind them that can accommodate the needs their clients have on a global basis.

Having these resources is necessary, but it isn't sufficient. You're not an effective banker if you can't deliver those resources to your client. Nothing is more important to maintaining a bond of trust with a client than delivering what you promise – "delivering the firm." So to be an effective advocate for your client, you must also build credibility within your own organization. The hub-and-spokes approach we use is an effective way to involve all of a firm's specialists in the client process, which helps cement those relationships. A culture that encourages open lines of communication within the firm is also essential. In addition, a good firm has an appetite for prudent risk and recognizes that part of its business is to take risks on behalf of its best clients.

In one recent high-profile example, our firm and a competitor were jointly advising a client on a complex acquisition that required a substantial commitment of resources and capital. The other investment bank had a strong relationship with the client, but in the end – despite assurances – they were unable to deliver their firm's resources (capital) to complete the deal. This put the client in an extremely precarious position. Fortunately, our bank was able to stand up for the capital deficit, and the client consummated the merger. In the end the client completed a very profitable transaction; we were able to syndicate the bulk of our exposure to other lenders; and our client was indebted to us because we not only delivered on our promise, but we also stepped up in his time of crisis.

Ask for the Order

Your team has done everything it was supposed to do. All the building blocks are in place. Your work is so thorough that you can predict which clients will do deals and when, and you are well-positioned with each one. Now the trick is to persevere and win the mandates.

Often mandates are preemptively awarded to the investment banks who have served the client best, but sometimes they go to firms for a variety of other reasons. Either way, investment banking is an extremely competitive business. Good bankers aggressively ask for mandates and don't leave anything to chance.

Asking for business can have many components. First, you must pitch your firm's credentials *(e.g.,* league tables, important transactions, research capabilities) to establish credibility in the transaction at hand. Keep in mind, the perception of your position relative to the firms you are competing against is what matters most, so it is important for you to control this flow of information to the client.

Second, your team must try to stay in front of the client and continually offer helpful advice and feedback. As a transaction gets closer to being launched, the level of detail the client must confront will increase exponentially *(e.g.,* covenant discussions, time lines, rating agency implications, dealing with commercial banking relationships, analyst reactions). This is a great opportunity to insert yourself into the discussion, add value, and raise the level of dialogue. Of course, there is an ulterior motive for staying in front of a client before decision time: If they are with you, then they aren't with your competition.

Finally, you must ask for the order at all levels of the organization, especially at the CEO and board-of-directors level, where the appropriate relationships exist. You must be specific and ask for what you desire; companies have many relationships to balance. Make sure they know exactly what you want *(e.g.,* bookrunner vs. co-lead, advisor vs. underwriter, minimum fee expectations) to avoid unnecessary disappointment later on.

Once, while waiting for an important loan and bond mandate to be awarded, our banking team sent the client an internal magazine article trumpeting our firm's capabilities in that area. The bankers drew quotation bubbles into the pictures in the article with comments like, "Gee, I sure hope we get to bookrun this new deal for ____." The correspondence accomplished many of our objectives – and injected levity into a tense situation.

It bears repeating: Investment banking is a team sport. Every individual has an important role to play, but we rely on each other to win. Anticipating trends, prioritizing clients, building relationships, generating ideas, delivering what you promise, and asking for the order are all rooted in the efforts of a team working together.

Richard Byrne is head of Debt Products and Financial Sponsors at Deutsche Bank and a member of the firm's Global Corporate Finance Operating Committee. In his current role he oversees Leveraged Finance, High Yield Capital Markets, Syndicated Lending, Structured Lending, and Project Finance, as well as Financial Sponsor Coverage. He also coordinates corporate coverage by the firm's debt bankers. Mr. Byrne joined Deutsche Bank in 1999, just as the firm was completing its acquisition of Bankers Trust, to help integrate the two firms.

Before joining Deutsche Bank, Mr. Byrne was co-head of the Global Leveraged Finance Group and Head of Global Credit Research at Merrill Lynch. He also was a perennially top-ranked credit analyst in numerous categories, most notably in the gaming, lodging, and leisure sector.

Mr. Byrne earned an MBA degree from Kellogg Graduate School of Management at Northwestern University and a BA from the State University of New York at Binghamton.

MIDDLE MARKET INVESTMENT BANKING: SERVICING THIS MARKET WITH SENIOR-LEVEL PROFESSIONALS

OLIVER D. CROMWELL

Bentley Associates LP

Senior Managing Director

Successful Investment Banking: The Individual and the Firm

Many investment banking firms define themselves as working in "the middle market." At major Wall Street firms this definition can encompass some relatively large corporate clients, so I think it is important from the outset to establish a definition for the context of this chapter. Although the senior professionals at our firm have all worked with large companies at various points in their careers – and are perfectly capable of servicing such companies today – we typically define our market by minimum deal size, rather than by the revenues or profits of our client companies. In our realm, we work with middle market companies that are looking either to raise $5 million or more from a private placement, private equity, or mezzanine financing, or to sell their business for $10 million or more.

The Individual

To be a successful investment banker in this marketplace, a person has to have a good ability to assess which transactions are most likely to be completed and brought to closure. This skill comes from many years in the business. Our typical investment banker has been in the business for more than 20 years and has seen a lot of deals, both that closed and that encountered problems. To put this important initial assessment process in perspective, we must always consider the investment parameters of the private equity funds that invest in the deals where our firm serves as an agent on behalf of our corporate client. Most of these private equity funds have told us they will invest in about one deal out of every hundred they review. So as we pick our clients for our capital-raising projects, we must be diligent. We also know that even making 100 phone calls will not get a deal done if it is the wrong deal. So the first element of success is the ability to make a sound initial assessment of the project.

The next step toward success is making sure the investment banking team has the required skill sets to be competent in the execution of the selected deals. Ideally, the investment banker should be familiar with the client's industry, as well as with the typical terms that occur in such deals, either in the private equity market or on an M&A transaction. At our firm, we have recruited senior-level professionals with industry expertise in a number of the most important industries in which a high proportion of deals are done, such as healthcare, media, real estate, consumer, technology, software, and financial institutions. At the same time we have made a real point of hiring industry generalists. As we see many businesses that are not in these special industry categories, it is also important to have people with broad general experience in a wide variety of transactions in many industries. To successfully execute transactions, we also find it very helpful to have transaction specialists. We have people who focus purely on the private placement market. They have cultivated excellent contact lists of potential investors, and they know the key terms in private mezzanine and equity deals. A second type of transaction specialist is the investment banker with M&A

expertise, who knows the typical terms of M&A deals. These markets and terms change over time, and frequently our industry-focused investment bankers will team with one of our product specialists to successfully execute a transaction.

Since we raise money almost exclusively from the institutional private equity and mezzanine markets, rather than the public markets, we constantly seek to understand the status of these private markets. For example, at each of our weekly group meetings during the year, we try to bring in a guest speaker from one of these funds. About 400 private funds have made presentations to our firm in the past 11 years. As a result, we not only keep apprised of issues and general market conditions, but also learn about specific investment criteria for that particular equity fund. An additional key benefit of these presentations is that we gain good access to that equity fund, which can be important to a boutique firm that does not benefit from the cachet of a major Wall Street name. If a fund invests in only one deal in every hundred, and if they are unfamiliar with Bentley's quality as a firm, we might not get the appropriate attention in their reviews of our deals. So these meetings serve the dual purposes of making sure we are very familiar with their fund, and giving us access when we call the fund with a deal. For example, we have heard from a professional at one of the major funds getting 30 to 40 e-mailed business plans a day. We asked how he even began to sort through so many business plans. He replied that his "first cut" was to eliminate all the e-mails from people or firms unknown to him.

The Firm

To be successful, the investment banker must pick the right deals, know the proper sources of capital, and then have good access to these institutions, based on both their own and their firm's reputations.

Turning from the factors that make an individual successful to those elements that help a firm succeed, one of the most important ingredients is making sure the firm adds and retains the right people. There is a certain profile, both personally and professionally, that we seek at Bentley. We have promised our middle market clients they will get senior-level attention on their projects for deals that typically fall a little below the threshold of the major Wall Street firms. As a result, to be successful in our firm's environment, where most people have 20 or more years of experience at major Wall Street firms, we seek people with a minimum of 10 years' experience. Also, I look for people who have a strong entrepreneurial spirit. They have to be a bit of an entrepreneur themselves, and given the way we operate as a firm, they must have a mindset similar to those of our clients, who are often entrepreneurs. Our investment bankers have worked extensively with middle market companies in the past and understand how these companies operate, appreciating both their strengths and weaknesses, as companies and as people. In addition to this entrepreneurial spirit, which in some instances could lead to selfish individualism, I also look for people who can fit in with our collegial style of operation and contribute in this environment, where two-person teams handle most projects.

Apart from the personality traits that help our professionals work with our clients and within the firm, we clearly need certain professional investment banking skill-sets. We can always use people who understand a particular industry or have mastered a certain function, such as private placements or M&A. Nevertheless, I have also made sure we have many "generalists," without expertise in any one industry, but with a very good Rolodex and working knowledge of investment banking deals, both in the private placement market and the M&A world. This formula of personal and professional skills has worked well since, at this point, we have lost no one in over two-and-a-half years.

Second, in addition to having good investment bankers for deal execution, it is vital to have a good source of business leads, so that the firm has good supply of potential projects. In that regard I have established relationships with five major Wall Street firms, which send us investment banking referrals for deals that are just below their deal-size thresholds. I established many of these key relationships just after founding the firm in my living room 11 years ago, having just had experience at a major firm that considered such deals uneconomic. These relationships have provided an excellent flow of potential leads for us to contemplate over the past six to 10 years that we have worked with each firm.

Third, in an environment where we are one of many boutique firms, I think it is very important for us to maintain a good reputation in the market. We would not be on five bulge-bracket firms' referral lists if we had any issues with our reputation, in terms of both integrity and professional skills. I continue to spend much of my time making sure those relationships are maintained and cultivated, whatever changes happen at these major firms, so they continue to send us business.

Last, for a firm to be successful, attention must be paid to the infrastructure necessary for getting deals closed, without ever forgetting that the appropriate databases and telecommunications and computer equipment are a means, not an end, in getting these deals closed. I try to respond to the needs of our investment bankers, but within the confines of our limited resources as a boutique. Specifically, we need adequate sources of information for our people and sufficient telecommunications infrastructure. On a daily basis, my role at the firm includes certain internal administrative and managerial functions that come as a result of being the one person at the firm who is not doing deals on a daily basis. At the same time, my primary function is still sourcing new business for the firm. I need to try to balance my time to ensure that the deal flow, the people, and the infrastructure are all in place for the firm to succeed.

The "Art" of Investment Banking

I believe the "art" of investment banking is in understanding the different nuances of each transaction, and then tailoring your service based on this understanding that comes from many years in the business. In each transaction the "art" comes into play based on what the client is trying to accomplish, within the context of their company and industry, and where they are in the process before the investment bankers get started on a project.

So the art of investment banking is taking a potential project, whether an M&A or financing assignment, starting to devise an execution plan based on industry deal norms and, more important, custom tailoring your approach based on what has transpired with the company, its goals, and the current market conditions. For example, on a merger assignment, certain features of the company may affect how you best position it for potential buyers, and these features may very well be different from a typical deal. When an investment banker is doing a financing or M&A transaction for a company, there is no single way to bring out the best features because each company and its situation is unique.

Also, apart from the specific company issues, aspects of the deal itself require a certain art. For instance, because confidentiality is sometimes of the utmost importance, a broad auction process would be very disruptive to business. Companies in that position can be shown to only one or two potential acquirers at a time. In such cases, there is a certain art to how the investment banker goes about the sale process itself.

Finally, on the personal level, there is something of an art to the negotiating process. I think some investment bankers are better negotiators in both procuring business for their firm in the first place and negotiating on behalf of their client once they are engaged on a project. Many of the people at our firm were at boutiques before joining Bentley, and they have a certain repository of knowledge about how to procure business and successfully close deals in the middle market without a huge support staff. We believe that this artistry, honed on prior deals and over the course of many years, can be shared for the benefit of others at our firm. One reason senior level professionals join us is for the opportunity to gain general deal input, or suggestions on how to handle a specific set of circumstances, from fellow professionals at the firm. People regularly come to me to discuss issues, such as how to craft an engagement letter to cover a variety of potential outcomes on an assignment, or to learn who I know at a particular firm that could help us determine whether a proposed alternative approach might be successful on a given deal.

Judging Success in Investment Banking

A boutique firm typically gets hired when a client has a specific transaction, usually either a capital-raising project or M&A transaction. Judging the success of a deal might initially appear to be a bimodal assessment, based solely on whether the deal closed – but it is not quite that simple. Obviously, a certain amount of success on a private placement occurs if the investment banker raises the money on the company's behalf. Yet, if onerous terms are included in the financing package, and the investment banker failed to properly alert the client to these important covenants, the deal may not be a long-term success. For example, a company failing to meet such covenants might encounter problems with the loan that could be very harmful to the company's operation. Another example might involve how, under certain circumstances, a venture capitalist could have the ability to effectively take over ownership of the company if certain performance requirements were not met. The investment banker may have raised the money, but would not have been as successful as he could have been if he had negotiated better terms or alerted the client to some of the nuances of the key deal terms. With experience in such fields, a successful investment banker can provide solid advice about these crucial issues that go beyond simply whether the deal is closed. Similarly, for real success on M&A transactions, it is essential that all the fundamental issues are properly addressed, such as the key terms and conditions, management team issues, compensation agreements and earn-out provisions in place, how the deal was financed, and a variety of other issues that go beyond closing.

Finally, a certain amount of the investment banker's success comes from whether the client was pleased with the overall process and the eventual outcome of the project. For example, last year we had a client project to raise $10million to $15 million in a very difficult environment for a relatively early-stage company in the technology arena. Ultimately, rather than receiving funding for a minority stake in the company from a private equity fund, the client was acquired by a large public company that will provide financing to grow the company. This outcome was not what the company had originally intended, but being acquired was ultimately the right move for the client. Ideally, in a successful deal the client is pleased with both the final outcome and the deal process itself.

On every deal the investment banker will find certain sticking points. You never know what they will be or when they will happen, although you do know from the outset that some problems will always occur and each one, and its solution, will be different. Once again, the art of investment banking comes into play as the senior banker handles these issues. Client companies remember the process as well as the outcome, often deciding whom they will work with in the future based on how well the investment banker handled the more problematic periods of previous deals.

Judging the "success" of a financing or M&A assignment, the investment banker obviously does have some initial feedback on a deal closing, which is clearly important in assessing whether a deal was successful. To make the final judgment on these projects, however, takes a little more time.

Investment Banking in the Middle Market

To further distinguish investment banking in the middle market from other markets, it is best to describe the types of projects we execute, as opposed to those that fall outside our scope, either below our segment or above it. With regard to smaller, very early-stage companies, as a firm we do not raise start-up capital from individual "angel" investors, which is the appropriate funding source for the under–$5 million financing level. Also, most institutional investors have little interest in investing in very early-stage companies, such as those that have only a few executives, are building their product prototype, or are doing the first rollout of their products. A financing in that market tends to be very labor intensive for the agent. The agents or investment bankers on such projects are likely to be very actively involved in the company, writing what amounts to their first business plan and actually developing the business, all while trying to find the financing from individual investors.

In our sector of the middle market, we normally become involved when the company is looking for its first or second institutional placement with the private equity funds. These companies typically have a full management team in place, and the business will be up and running, with a relatively proven track record and a certain amount of revenues. The amount of revenues can vary widely depending on the industry, and we can work effectively with some industries that have lower revenues than others. For example, comparing a software company to a wholesale distribution company, we could work with a low-revenue software company because of the high profit margins and excellent growth prospects, as well as with a large distribution company that has razor-thin margins and low growth prospects. After the dot-com shakeout, private equity funds again raised their thresholds. We, too, are looking to represent companies that have some positive cash flow as they seek their first institutional round. And finally, in our sector the investment bankers deal strictly at the CEO level, with people who are very frequently the owners, operators, and founders of their companies.

One essential difference between a boutique and a larger firm working in the very upper-end of the middle market is the latter's huge infrastructure and staff, which can be a mixed blessing for a client company. At our firm, we have only senior people, who actually stay involved and work with the clients directly throughout the course of the project. At the larger firms, there is a correspondingly larger work force, so that smaller deals are actually executed by more junior people. Only on the larger, more lucrative deals will the top investment bankers stay actively involved. In addition to staffing differences, we are typically the only investment banker on a project; whereas, at the larger firms, they more frequently do deals jointly with other investment banks. On an M&A assignment, if the owner is going to sell his or her business, this will likely be a one-time project for the boutique. By comparison, a large company using a larger investment banking firm might sell this division this year and another division the next, generating repeat business for the larger firm.

Specific Strategies

One of the core strategies for our successful operation in this very competitive middle market segment has been our relationships with the major Wall Street firms that refer projects to us that fall below their thresholds. We are on the referral list of these five firms because we have an excellent reputation, because we have the critical mass of senior level professionals who have done deals in every kind of industry, and because we are not considered a specialist firm. Also, because our firm has 20 senior-level investment bankers, these referral firms do not have to remember that we specialize in any one area or worry that we will lack the capacity to review their potential deals and execute their transactions. Moreover, we do not compete with these major firms for the public offerings and the deals we are doing are below their thresholds. As a result, they find it a real benefit to be able to send us deals that fall below their threshold, so they can still indirectly service their earlier-stage clients, and not just tell these prospective future clients that they cannot be of assistance.

Bentley also benefits by being able to use these major firms on our reference list, though we are very careful not to use their names in our written material. Being brought in as an official third-party referral firm gives us a certain "positive glow" by association with the referring firm. Interestingly, each of these major-bracket firms is comforted by the knowledge that we are also actively working with other similar firms, because it demonstrates our extensive experience in handling such referrals. When the referral comes in for my initial review, I get enough information about the company and the potential project to determine whether it makes sense for us to investigate and begin to pursue it. About 90 percent of the time a referral is given further review by either an industry or a transaction specialist. After they look at the situation in more depth, they make the independent decision as to whether they want to become engaged.

An important element of our corporate strategy relates to the internal operation of our firm. Specifically, our senior people receive the highest payouts on Wall Street, as a percentage of fees, for their projects. These senior executives do not draw a salary and cover a modest portion of the firm's shared expenses. For that trade-off, they keep an extremely large portion of the fees generated. We have pushed certain expenses down to the individual level and, at the same time, have given people a very high payout for superior performance. A predetermined formula for splitting fees eliminates potential revenue-sharing problems that plague many firms. We usually operate in two-person teams, matching an industry specialist with a private placement/M&A specialist, although some teams have two members with complementary skill sets in a given industry.

Keeping an Edge in Investment Banking

Keeping an edge in this industry has three principal components: continuously increasing and improving deal flow, attracting and retaining good people, and keeping current with key trends that could affect your business.

You keep an edge by staying in touch with the people who are most important to making your business thrive – in our case, the referral firms. By monitoring their current organizational structure, their changing needs, and our response in helping them reach their goals, we keep our edge over any potential competitors. I try to stay focused on the classic 80-20 rule of thumb, concentrating on the 20 percent that provide our firm with the most business. At the same time, I also try to cast a wide net for leads by employing such techniques as mass-mailings (still with a personal note on each cover letter) to the names on my business mailing list. Each year I am pleasantly surprised by the number of referrals that come from people I have not spoken with for several years, but who now have a deal idea that may be of interest to our firm.

The Future of Investment Banking

One of the primary changes of the recent past is that the increasing availability and sophistication of technology is acting as a great equalizer, giving boutique firms access to information that only the major firms could have obtained in the past. Not only is information available on the Web, but we also subscribe to an incredible database, which details about 7,000 private equity funds and 50,000 portfolio companies. As a result, our boutique firm can be just as sophisticated as the major bracket firms with the kind of proprietary database we could never have afforded to maintain alone. The technology levels the playing field, allowing boutiques to compete with larger firms on deals. I see technology continuing to narrow the historical resource gap between smaller and larger firms.

Second, since I started my career in the mid-1970s, the major firms have massively expanded staffing levels. They do serve a useful function in meeting the needs of large multinationals. However, in the next five to 10 years there will continue to be a place for boutique firms like ours because middle market clients do want a certain amount of senior level attention for their deals. Despite the potential cachet of having a recognized name as their investment bank, these middle market companies do not want their financing project or the sale of their business to be "a practice exercise" for a new associate just out of business school. Most owner/entrepreneurs have built their businesses over a lifetime, and they both want and deserve a senior person to execute their most important transactions. As the major firms stay very large, I think there will continue to be a good number of boutique firms like ours that can thrive below their high thresholds, particularly under the internal compensation scheme that works at our firm.

Oliver D. Cromwell is the senior managing director and founder of Bentley Associates, an investment banking firm working with middle market companies since 1991. Mr. Cromwell first worked for Bankers Trust Company in 1973 and 1974. He began his investment banking career at Donaldson, Lufkin & Jenrette in 1976. He was promoted to vice president in 1980 and to senior vice president in 1985. In 1987 he joined the Corporate Finance Department of Oppenheimer and moved to the Investment Banking Group of PaineWebber in 1988. Throughout his investment banking career, he has been a generalist working on a wide variety of transactions for middle market companies in many different industries.

Mr. Cromwell was on the Executive Committee of the Board of Governors of the Securities Industry Association (New York District), and has earned a Chartered Financial Analyst (CFA) designation. He has been a panel moderator and speaker at numerous conferences involving investment banking issues.

Mr. Cromwell served two terms as president of the Brown University Club in New York from 1991 to 1993. He received his BA from Brown University in 1972 and his MBA from Harvard Business School in 1976.

INVESTMENT BANKING AND THE IMPORTANCE OF RELATIONSHIPS

JIMMY DUNNE, III

Sandler O'Neill & Partners, LP

Senior Managing Partner

Relationships Are Everything

Building relationships is the secret to success in the investment banking industry. A good investment banker builds a solid relationship with his clients by understanding their needs and by putting their agendas first. It is also critical to have a thorough understanding of various markets and strategic trends and the implications they will have on the client's decisions.

Personally, I enjoy establishing long-term, meaningful client relationships. I like being involved as my clients make critical decisions at seminal points in their companies' history. In this business there is an opportunity to deal one-on-one with what I call an institution's "spiritual leader." I like exchanging ideas on how these leaders can advance their business for the good of their customers, shareholders, and employees. Many of these decisions are the most important a client will make. When you are working with people with whom you have a long-term relationship, there is an intense personal, as well as professional, pressure to be right. It's not like selling ice cream on the corner.

My goal is to give a client everything our firm has to offer. I want every client to be so satisfied with the quality and depth of our service that they recommend our firm to their peers. In the end, a reference means our clients feel they received the highest-quality service and advice from us. And if we end up with a reference, it's a good gauge that we have done well financially.

Weathering a Turbulent Economy

Sandler O'Neill's emphasis on long-term relationships has helped us weather turbulent times. We actually tend to outperform our competition when we are not in the uproar of an economic boom. Business opportunities exist whether the economy is good or bad. A good investment banker's working relationship doesn't rely on a booming economy – it relies on the quality of advice and level of trust he or she offers the client. A great economy simply provides more chances to capitalize on opportunities. If a good investment banker has solid client relationships, he or she will still have a successful business, regardless of the overall strength of the economy.

The most challenging aspect of the investment banking business is working with volatile markets in unstable times. Investment banking is highly competitive and involves a fair amount of pressure and risk. It demands an intense focus for long periods of time.

In a turbulent economy some investment banks lose focus. Some will move away from long-term, relationship-driven business toward short-term, transactional business. While all investment banks want to be involved in transactions, it is critical to maintain a long-term perspective, even if it means foregoing a fee. Over the long run, this decision will bear more fruit than one made for short-term gain. A long-term view, integrity, and persistence will have greater ramifications than a specific quarterly report.

Industry Focus: A Critical Aspect of Investment Banking

Sandler O'Neill works solely with financial institutions – ranging from the smallest community banks to the largest bank holding companies. Because we are completely focused on financial institutions, we avoid the impulse to jump into other sectors that might be hot at the time. Our firm's expertise is spread across the full spectrum of investment banking service lines, including fixed-income trading, asset/liability analysis, sales and equity trading, research, and capital markets. Our firm does not restrict itself to one area of business, such as mergers and acquisitions. In fact, we believe it's more valuable to advise a client for three or four years, help them build a better franchise and interact with them at every level of business. This way, we work with a company to help build a more valuable entity and heighten the possibility of doing a transaction or sale that's more valuable to everyone involved. We look at each situation as unique and make sure our agenda is not set before the relationship starts.

In terms of transactions, Sandler O'Neill is involved in capital markets, mergers and acquisitions, and mortgage finance transactions. Unlike most companies, we are involved in every aspect of a company's balance sheet. We are narrow in our industry focus, but broad in our discipline.

Our firm focuses on the client, their industry, and their needs. We don't want just to sell a particular expertise; we want to understand the company's long-term plan and how we can augment it through a variety of different services. Given the depth of our industry coverage, smaller clients get more attention from us than they would from larger institutions.

People do business with us because of our experience in the sector and the quality of our relationships. We've always felt that a smart client was our best client. Because we are a niche firm, it takes a smart person to say, "Listen, this might not be a well-known name, but they know everything that's going on in my sector. They are dedicated to my sector. I trust them and know them and understand how important this deal is. I'm going to hire them for this task, rather than just hiring a name my board recognizes." There are highly talented people in high-profile firms, but we've always felt smart clients will hire us because they appreciate the benefits of our expertise.

Essentials of a Good Investment Banker

To be successful advising companies on mergers and acquisitions, an investment banker must have credibility, integrity, analytical and people skills, and the realization that all good deals involve some give and take. A good investment banker understands the balance between playing hardball and knowing when to compromise. If an investment banker wants too much control or has an unrealistic outlook for the value of the company, there is a good chance he or she will not be successful for very long.

If an investment banker identifies a company with an outstanding management team, then he or she might try to join them with another company that would value its capabilities. The banker would closely study the client's performance and the history of its balance sheet. It is important to examine key lines of business, such as the loan portfolio, and determine how well the company controls credit, finances, and technology. If an investment banker spends a couple of hours discussing these topics with the management team, he or she will get an initial sense of where the company is positioned and where they are going.

When valuing a company from a buyer's or seller's perspective, we consider a variety of things. We examine who they are, who they want to be, and how successful they've been in fulfilling these goals. We look at their earnings per share growth, the business opportunities in their market, and reasons someone would want to acquire them or be acquired by them. In addition, we consider whether they are taking the steps necessary to make the company more valuable in five years. Are they maximizing their potential – expanding their geographic footprint, increasing their returns, growing the customer base? In short, are they enhancing shareholder value?

Public Versus Private Companies

Public and private companies differ greatly. A public company has more disclosure and accountability to a broader base than a traditional private company. This is not to say that one is better than the other. A private company doesn't have to answer to as many people or worry as much about quarter-to-quarter results. In a public company many more people demand answers, but a currency allows the company flexibility to do more than it could if it were private. We often advise companies to go public because it gives them a currency to compete in the mergers and acquisitions world and allows them to grow through transactions.

When making the transition from a private to a public company, there are very different demands. It's not guaranteed that a good CEO of a private company will be diversified enough to be a good CEO of a public company. They are two very different breeds of cat.

Capital-Raising Criteria

I generally look at a few major criteria in companies that are evaluating an Initial Public Offering. I evaluate the need for capital and the importance of establishing a currency. It is also crucial to examine the management team and its ability to maximize the company's potential. A need for capital and a need for the currency, combined with a good management team, create a very powerful force.

A key to raising capital is defining a valuable and logical use for it. Each company needs a plan that demonstrates a specific need for a specific type of capital to do a specific type of business. Perhaps the company's earnings per share growth limits its expansion opportunities that might come through mergers and acquisitions. If a well-run company can demonstrate a logical purpose for capital, and demonstrate that the cost of that capital is economical, it will have access to the capital markets. A company will have difficulty if it does not have a good explanation or good history of using capital wisely.

The investment banker should also examine whether the client has a very strong financial person to manage the capital, whether it has a technology plan that will anticipate the needs of its customers going forward, and finally, whether it has the right credit person to make the correct risk/reward decisions. He or she should also consider who would replace these people in the longer term and what the plan is for succession.

Value Investing

Behind the most sophisticated investment banking models and complicated capital transactions are emotional people with their own levels of greed, anxiety, and fear. The failure of the dot-coms exemplifies a mistake that has been made over and over again, although the failure is more dramatic because more people have been affected to greater extremes.

Wall Street is so interesting because people are driven by a variety of different motivators. This tends to exaggerate market moves on both the upside and the downside. That is when the difference between value investing and growth investing becomes very evident. While there are periods where it seems tedious to invest in value, over time there is a consistent reward in smart, long-term investing.

Key to Any Successful Business: Quality People

To create a successful business, a company needs people who are creative, work hard, and compete with class. There are a lot of these people in this business.

A leader must have a strong work ethic and the ability to articulate complicated issues in simple language. A good leader needs to cut to the core of an issue, keep sight of what's important, and walk away from a deal that's not right. He or she must be willing to learn, listen, and have real pride, but not a big ego.

A successful team requires an owner-like mentality: Every person should feel they own a piece of the ultimate product and process. A company is successful when everyone knows they are responsible for making sure the company provides the highest-quality product. The interests of the client supersede those of any individual who might want to put his or her own brand or mark on it. Cooperation is necessary – from the highest level all the way down to the people who process the information.

A leader at an investment bank should hire people who enjoy the battle and the volatility of Wall Street. Then he or she should find people who can learn quickly, think on their feet, and think out of the box. It is important that they have incentive, so that they enjoy what they are doing and know they will be duly compensated. Good investment bankers need to have both the love of the game and the incentive to win, or they'll never be great. Even the greats, if they stop loving it, will stop doing it. It's a lot of pressure.

The golden rules of investment banking are simple: Tell the truth. Maintain confidentiality. Maintain integrity. Work hard to stay on the cutting edge of the trends and issues in your marketplace. Know your clients – understand how they feel; you're in a relationship business. Behind all these deals are people. Don't get too far away from understanding that. Finally, always put the client's interests first – well ahead of any fee. If you advice a client *not* to do a deal that would generate a fee for you but would not give them long-term value, they will love you for it and never forget it.

Jimmy Dunne, III, is the senior managing partner of Sandler O'Neill & Partners, LP, a full-service investment banking firm that provides innovative advisory and transaction execution services to the financial industry, with offices in New York, Boston, Chicago, and San Francisco.

Mr. Dunne's career on Wall Street spans more than 20 years. It began in 1978 with L.F. Rothschild's Bank Service Group, where he worked with financial institutions. He joined Lehman Brothers as a government securities trader in 1982; ultimately he was in charge of long-term U.S. Treasury trading commitments. In 1984 he joined

Prudential Bache in the same capacity, and two years later he became part of Bear Stearns' Financial Services Group. Mr. Dunne was appointed an associate director at Bear Stearns in 1987 and a senior sales manager in 1988.

In August 1988 the senior management team of Bear Stearns' Financial Services Group formed Sandler O'Neill & Partners, LP. As one of the founders of the firm, Mr. Dunne also serves as a member of Sandler O'Neill's Executive Committee.

Mr. Dunne received his BA in economics from the University of Notre Dame.

Before September 11, 2001, Sandler O'Neill's headquarters were located on the 104th floor of Two World Trade Center, and the firm had a total of 171 people in its offices nationwide. On September 11, the firm lost 66 people – including two of the three people who ran the firm, Herman Sandler and Chris Quackenbush. Mr. Dunne supervised the rapid recovery process of Sandler O'Neill and appointed two partners – Fred Price and Jon Doyle –

to operate the firm with him as principals. To date, Sandler O'Neill has hired more than 60 new people for its various business units. On January 22, 2002, Sandler O'Neill re-instituted full market marking operations in its new headquarters in Midtown Manhattan.

COMPANIES IN DISTRESS: WHEN RESTRUCTURING IS THE ANSWER

MARK E. CHESEN

SSG Capital Advisors, LP

President

Restructuring Investment Banking: An Overview

One of my mentors told me long ago the key to success in investment banking is to underwrite the situation on the front end. If you take on the right clients, you will be successful in getting your deals done. When a prospective client comes to you, it boils down to underwriting a situation – determining whether a deal can be done: Can it be refinanced or restructured or sold? That is the first question to ask any time a new opportunity presents itself. Also, are the investment bankers and the company on the same wavelength? Do we think the company is worth about the same amount of money? Do we have the same ideas for how the private placement should be structured? This underwriting discipline is important because we get a lot of prospective clients; we have to make sure the prospective client company is not so far gone that we are unable to help. It is something you learn over time. As a young investment banker you try to take every opportunity that comes across your desk, but with experience you learn it is better to spend time, effort, and money up front, before being retained, to assess the likelihood of getting a deal done.

To achieve a successful restructuring, you need professionals who can think on their feet. In selling or helping a company that is facing challenges, the solution on Day One may be to sell the entire business; several months into the process the company could be in freefall, and you may have to sell multiple divisions of the company to several separate buyers instead of selling it all to one buyer. You may find you cannot sell the company, and you have to restructure the business. You may start in a refinancing mode and see things go horribly awry for some reason. You have to think on your feet and perform well under pressure.

You report indirectly to multiple stakeholders – who include everyone from the owners to the lenders, to the customers who are not happy with where the company stands, to the suppliers – and you have to be a voice of reason in this process. You are part investment banker and part rabbi/priest/social worker, making sure your clients keep their faith and telling them there is light at the end of the tunnel. Your clients are in a difficult situation and should not take things personally when banks are calling in their loans and when customers, suppliers, and employees may be unhappy. We try to have our clients offload much of the communication with the various stakeholders on us, the investment bankers. We try to focus our clients on running their day-to-day business. A lot of what we do with our clients is trying to make sure we understand their goals – which may include paying off creditors, getting off contingent liabilities, maintaining an employment arrangement going forward, and so on.

To be successful in this business, the most critical thing is to remember that all you have is your individual and firm reputation. It's important to do your due diligence up front, do your underwriting up front, and make sure you are on the same wavelength as your prospective client. The last thing you want to do is take on an assignment in which you should have known from day one that you could not achieve your client's objectives. Second, take on only those assignments that are your core competency.

Restructuring Investment Banking – The Process

Restructuring investment bankers assist clients in achieving their goals with regard to buying, selling, refinancing, or restructuring businesses in transition that are facing challenging situations. Companies in transition include those facing legal, financial, and operational challenges. Investment bankers get retained, for example, in a situation where a company is facing a crisis, and their lender or other creditors are putting pressure on them to consider refinancing, restructuring, or selling all or part of their business to help solve the challenges at hand. The creditor's primary concern is getting their principal back; however, that may conflict with the company's objectives, which are to keep the company alive, maintain full employment, and grow the business. A lender may say, "We want our money back, and we don't care what you do with business." In those situations it can be challenging to accomplish the goals of the company, while at the same time assisting in maximizing recovery for the creditors of the company.

Restructuring investment bankers act as an insurance policy for our companies in crisis. Most businesses that are facing major hurdles are doing their best to keep their companies alive day to day. At times, companies need to retain the outside services of a professional who knows how to simultaneously pursue refinancing, restructuring, or selling all or part of a business that finds itself in trouble. Most businesses find themselves in trouble for the first time, and need a roadmap to avoid the pitfalls along the way to financial recovery.

Restructuring investment banking tends to be counter-cyclical to the overall economy. When the economy is healthy, the restructuring world tends to be more steady state, as rising tides keep many ships afloat that may not be seaworthy. In contrast, when the economy goes into recession, restructuring situations are plentiful.

Reporting Information – Full Disclosure!

When it comes to anything in life, honesty is the best policy, and investment banking is no exception. Companies facing challenges need to provide their key lender and investors with up-to-the-minute information, whether it's good news or not so good news. Lenders and investors can make informed decisions and react in a more rational manner if they have the facts in front of them promptly. Our motto is to provide both current and prospective lenders and investors with the good, the bad, and the ugly that describes the company in complete detail. If the company chooses not to pass along negative information, it is bound to come out at some point in time anyway, and at that point, it will destroy all of management's credibility.

The Restructuring Game Plan

Financing Alternatives

When the overall economy is healthy, and a company is facing a challenging situation, refinancing their way out of the problem can be an effective means to get a company back on its feet.

When a company seeks to raise capital, investment bankers meet with the executive team to assess the probability of raising capital. It is important to make sure everyone is on the same wavelength on the front end of a project. Two fundamental questions to research at the start of any assignment are whether the financing is viable for a given set of circumstances, and whether the prospective client is realistic about the rates, terms, and structure of the proposed financing.

For example, if a company wants to raise $25 million in equity, and the investment banker believes they can do so, that would answer the first question. But if a prospective client wants to give up no more than 10 percent ownership, and the investment banker believes, after thorough research, they have to give up 50 percent, this may not be an assignment the professional investment banker should take on.

There are a number of different ways to raise capital. Senior debt involves loans made to a company in which the company borrows from a bank, commercial finance company, insurance company, or other lender, and the lender is primarily earning a return on interest and fees charged to the borrower. The financing source ultimately expects to get paid back the principal amount of the loan at a stated maturity date. Subordinated debt with warrants, or mezzanine debt, on the other hand, is a hybrid instrument with both debt and equity features, in which a financing source lends a company, expecting to earn money in the form of interest and fees, as well as in sharing in the equity of the company. In this method this lender is junior to a senior lender in the capital structure of the company. A subordinated debt, or mezzanine lender, ultimately expects to have their principal loan paid back, while an equity investment is an investment from an individual or institution investing in the common stock or preferred stock of the company. A substantial portion of the investor's return will come in the form of appreciation in the value of the company at the time the company is sold or refinanced or if it goes public, at some point in the future.

It is important for an investment banker to understand the goals of their clients. Are they debt-averse? Are they willing to give up equity? What does the balance sheet look like? We look at results and projections to determine the appropriate capital structure of the company. We then settle on a combination of senior or subordinated debt and equity that makes sense for the given situation. Some companies are asset rich and have receivables, inventory, or real estate on their balance sheet, and that might be conducive to an asset-based senior debt financing because asset-based lenders like to have collateral in the form of hard assets. A company without hard assets might be better with cash flow, senior debt facility, or sub-debt or equity.

Merger and Acquisition Alternatives

When the overall economy is in a tailspin, or a given industry is facing major issues, companies in distress tend to solve their problems through a sale of all or part of their businesses.

Restructuring investment bankers are involved in merger and acquisition deals, assisting both buyers and sellers in accomplishing their goals and objectives. Buy-side assignments involve representing buyers who want to acquire companies facing crises, while sell-side deals involve representing clients that want to sell all or part of their operations to help solve the challenges at hand. As an example, one recent M&A transaction we participated in was the representation of Baldwin Piano and Organ Company, an old established public company that had fallen on hard times and filed for Chapter 11 protection under the United States Bankruptcy Code. The senior lenders wanted their money back and wanted the company sold, restructured, or refinanced as a way of getting their loan repaid. Our firm was retained to represent Baldwin in helping them explore their strategic options, which ranged from refinancing or restructuring or selling the company. The assignment was taken on in late August 2001, immediately prior to the horror of September 11. Once the events of September 11 unfolded, financing and restructuring opportunities for the company were limited, and we focused on selling the business, while continuing to pursue both refinancing and restructuring alternatives for Baldwin. We concentrated on identifying both strategic buyers (companies that manufactured other musical instruments and might be interested in Baldwin) and financial buyers (such as equity groups that may or may not have had investments in the musical instrument industry, but that wanted to invest in a wide array of industries). We canvassed the marketplace and brought several potential buyers to the table. Ultimately the company was sold through a formal auction process under the direction of the United States Bankruptcy Court, to Gibson Guitar Corporation, which wanted to diversify their business and add a premier piano and organ company to their product mix. The senior lender accomplished their objective of getting their loan paid off in full, and the company was allowed to continue as a going concern.

Restructuring Alternatives

At times, in spite of the efforts of management and all of the stakeholders in the company, the lenders, bondholders, unsecured creditors, unions, and customers, a company may not be able to refinance its operation or sell all or part of the business to solve the challenges at hand. When that happens, the goal of the investment banker is to avoid the outright liquidation of the company. In most liquidation scenarios, nobody wins. At times, when refinancing and M&A alternatives are limited, a restructuring of existing obligations may lead to the maximum recovery for all stakeholders involved in the company. Examples may include lenders who are willing to convert all or a portion of their debt obligation from the company to equity; customers willing to enter into long-term purchasing agreements with the companies; suppliers willing to enter into long-term favorable supply agreements with the company; union employees and other employee groups willing to make short-term or long-term wage concessions in return for increased ownership in the business; and local, state, and federal governments willing to step in and help support a restructuring. A restructuring may not be number one on any stakeholder's list of preferred restructuring outcomes, but in most cases, when all other options have failed, it beats liquidation.

A Note About Management's Role in Restructuring

Management is critical in the successful completion of any type of investment banking assignment. There may be a combination of company management and consultants or crisis managers who guide the company through these uncharted waters. Restructuring investment bankers work with the current management team of a company in transition and assist in negotiating incentives for the management team to remain in place, in situations where there may be little opportunity for management to remain with the company in the long term.

Valuing a Company in Transition

Valuation of a company depends on the given company and the industry. In restructuring investment banking, it becomes difficult to use typical valuation methodologies to value a company that is in distress. For companies that are in trouble, valuation methodologies start at a premium to liquidation value, but not a substantial premium. For companies that are in a restructuring mode, buyers tend to focus on the asset side of a balance sheet and look at the tangible and intangible assets as the best way of valuing the company. If a company is being sold in a bankruptcy setting, it will usually go through a formal auction process, where potential buyers are made aware of an auction taking place in the United States Bankruptcy Court, and the end value will be what the auction generates.

As it relates to valuation, there are no major differences between a public and a private company in distress. Buyers will still look at the premium above a liquidation value for companies in distress. If they do not pay a premium, the current lenders and investors will decide to shut the company down, regardless of whether it is a public or private company.

There may be more of a distinction in valuations within a given industry. For example, our firm recently sold an independent television broadcasting station in a major United States market for 30 times revenue, 60 times cash flow. Even though the company was in distress and operating under Chapter 11 protection of the United States Bankruptcy Code, it had a license from the FCC to provide television broadcasts in the Washington, D.C., market, and a major strategic buyer wanted to obtain the license and reformat the programming to something completely different from what that company had been doing. Valuable intangible assets may generate a substantial premium, even if the company is operating in a restructuring environment.

Mark E. Chesen is one of four founding partners of SSG Capital Advisors, LP, and was cofounder of its predecessor, Berwind Financial, LP's Special Situations Group, and co-head of Berwind's Investment Banking Practice. Since 1995 Mr. Chesen has completed more than 80 financial restructuring investment banking assignments, involving the private placement of senior debt, subordinated debt, and equity capital for companies in a turnaround or transitional mode. In addition, he has extensive experience in selling and restructuring companies facing challenging situations, including companies operating under Chapter 11 protection of the United States

Bankruptcy Code. He has worked with clients in a wide array of industries, including many in the manufacturing, distribution, food processing, printing, telecommunication, and healthcare industries. Before joining Berwind Financial, Mr. Chesen was associated with Meridian Capital Markets as a vice president of Meridian's Investment Banking Group.

Mr. Chesen received his Bachelor of Science degree in accounting from the University of Texas in Austin and graduated with highest honors. He is a Certified Public Accountant, and his professional affiliations include membership in the Turnaround Management Association and the American Bankruptcy Institute. In addition, he is a member of the Advisory Board of the Commercial Financial Educational Foundation.

INVESTMENT BANKING:
A WALK IN THE WOODS

GERALD ROSENFELD

Rothschild North America, Inc.

Chief Executive Officer

Wearing Two Hats: Banker and Manager

The art of investment banking is a blending of financial skills and personal skills. It's a combination that enables a banker to gain a client's confidence on one hand, and provide substantive, value-added counsel – whether it's a financing or merger transaction – on the other.

One of the most rewarding aspects of this industry is the opportunity to participate in challenging transactions with interesting people. Many of these types of deals have never been done in exactly the same way before, so it's exciting to solve problems in new ways. You do this by listening to the client, finding out what he wants, and then using your experience and knowledge and to translate the problem-solving skills on the client's side to what is doable and feasible in the market. You create solutions for clients based on your experience and on listening to what the client has to say. For example, many clients will come in and say, "I'd like to grow my business but I'm constrained in terms of capital," or "I have a good business, but my balance sheet is overleveraged." You then translate that problem into the feasibility of either raising new capital or restructuring the debt that is already in place.

The most important component of what I do is on the people side. I am a manager, as well as a banker. I talk to the people here who are out serving the clients and help them think about their client businesses, making sure they are focused on the client. Given how our firm is growing, I also spend a lot of time meeting new people to see whether they can fit into our place. The second component of my work is talking to clients about active transactions. I spend some time talking to clients about the current status of their transactions and what steps have been taken. Third, I keep up a constant dialogue with other clients, those who may not be in the midst of a current transaction, about their overall business and where we may be able to help.

Being an active banker and manager at the same time has its benefits, but these benefits come at a cost. In terms of reinforcing the skills on both sides, working in both roles is very powerful. Talking to clients and being aware of and active in the business of our clients as a banker makes me a better manager. Moreover, using the experience I have built over the years to help the younger people here adds to the benefits. The difficult part is managing time. Being in the middle of a large transaction takes an enormous amount of time – it's hard to be a good manager when you are stuck in a conference room all day. The time flows between transactions and managerial jobs is difficult. The most challenging part of the job is managing your time so you can stay involved with the clients to the maximum extent possible.

The Valuation Trick: Seeing the Forest *and* the Trees

The biggest issue in all transactions is valuation. There are many instances in which there is a good strategic fit to a transaction, but the buyer and the seller cannot agree on valuation. Many times a good dialogue is established between the buyer and seller, but it does not end in a transaction because of differences in value thinking. Social issues are also tricky to work out. Making sure the various parties who need to be included in the deal can find their way into the management structure is a challenge.

Deals change largely because buyers and sellers don't have a good handle on value. In stable markets people can feel comfortable about valuation metrics. In turbulent economies, however, even deals that are well-structured and well-conceived founder because people are nervous and unsure about future conditions and value. The approach to a deal is the same in both stable and turbulent economies; however, you must be prepared to work harder and longer when conditions in the economy are unstable. It is simply more of the same approach, only done more delicately.

Valuation is more of an art than a science. There are standard methodologies people use, such as discounted cash flow and measurements on comparable companies. Good valuation skills take in all the inputs and methodologies and blend them together to find a transaction value both companies are willing to live with. The issue is finding common ground. The key things in valuation are being able to look into the future of the business and understanding the macroeconomic impacts that people may sometimes overlook – the bigger picture. For example, in valuing Microsoft in the early 1980s, if you did not have the vision of the PC revolution and did not know that Windows would be the standard operating system for the majority of businesses, if you were focusing on the company's cash flow for that week or the next quarter, you would have missed the real value of Microsoft.

Another part of M&A valuation relates to synergies brought to a transaction by the buyer. In M&A valuation, "What is this company worth?" is an incomplete question. The more complete question is, "What is this company worth to my client?" – a specific buyer. It is the difference in combination economics, revenue-driven, cost-driven, or both, that gives rise to different bids for the same company by different buyers.

Bankers need to be broader-based businesspeople who can move from the forest to the trees and back again. It is up to the banker to make sure the knowledge the client has of their company is integrated into the valuation and negotiation side of the transaction. The best bankers find a way to shuttle between the forest and the trees, taking both into account.

The methodologies for valuing private and public companies are the same, but for a public company, a lot more information is available. Many people every day buy and sell stock in the public company; those transactions provide a wealth of knowledge and input from these buyers and sellers. The trick in the case of a public company is to see what the market sees, or what you see on the stock market, and what determines what the next thousand shares will trade at, or what the last thousand traded at. You must be able to extrapolate the trading price of the company, which is about short-term trading value (the trees), into long-term M&A value (the forest). M&A is not just about the value of the company on its own, but its value to the buyer, because each buyer brings something different to the table. Each buyer brings to an M&A situation a different view of the future and a different ability to change the future of a particular company. It is different from a securities valuation because of the impact of what the buyer can bring to the table.

Raising Capital: Making a Good Marriage

IPOs are the most prominent part of equity capital – marrying good business models with an investment banking firm that understands the business and can help the company access institutional investors who are willing to provide capital. The banker needs to learn as much as possible about the company and understand the sustainability of the business model. Value creation and the business model, especially for smaller private companies, are the most important parts of raising equity capital. With the banker's help, the company executives write a story embodied in the registration statement and advertise to sources of capital around the world, searching for demand for that business model at the given valuation.

Secondary offers for public firms are slightly different because the story is already known, and the financial picture of the company has been public for while. This case is about pricing and determining whether there is demand for more shares in the company and, if so, how much demand. It is important for the investment banker to marry the demand for that company's shares with the institutional investors who both currently trade the stock and are prospective new owners. It is in some sense a continuation of the story that began with the IPO, but one that investment bankers have to bring to the institutional investment world in a systematic format that allows the seller, or company, to find a price at which new buyers are willing to invest.

The issue with debt capital is more about whether the debt will be paid back, rather than what the long-term growth value of the company is. It is fundamentally a different analysis. The question is whether the company in question has sufficient cash flow and prospects to be able to pay the money back. In both the public and private markets, fundamentally it is about credit. The investment banker works on behalf of the client to convince both the institutional investors who invest in debt and the debt-rating agencies that are credit-oriented that investing in the client is a good credit decision.

In the IPO world the biggest challenge for bankers is distinguishing among lots of people who would like to access these markets, and then determining which are good candidates for public markets and which are not. Once a banker and a company decide to work together, the next challenge is making sure there is a clear understating on both sides as to what the business model is, how it makes money, and what the risks are. The banker must do as good a job as he or she can to communicate that understanding to the institutional investor marketplace. Both the company and the banker need to communicate properly to one another to ensure they get the story right. From here, the banker has to convince investors of the story. He must choose whom to work with and understand the business well enough that he can communicate his understanding to the investors.

Overall, the uncertainty of the macroeconomic world in attempting to predict the future is the biggest challenge.

The Future of the Industry

Looking to the future, one question is whether the big banks with the big balance sheets will consolidate all the businesses to themselves. It is more likely, however, that the various parts of the financial services world will find their own places, and we will have a restructuring of the industry back into more specializations.

Right now we see commercial banks in investment banking; investment banks are lending money; M&A boutiques are trying to be merchant bankers...everyone is trying to do everything. It is likely that over the next few years we may see a return to people specializing in what they know how to do. For example, a number of commercial and big European banks thought they were going to be big investment bankers, but they are now beginning to pull back from that. Banks need to keep doing what they do well – although this is a minority view.

Success as an Investment Banker

An investment banker's most valuable skill is being able to apply experience from one situation to others, and getting clients and people from the other side of the table to trust your judgment and trust that what you seek is a transaction that works for both sides. You have to provide strong, solid advice for both sides and be skilled at solving problems.

It helps to be able to provide technical advice, as well. When two parties are having trouble reaching a deal because of one technicality or another, experience provides the ability to look back at similar situations where the same problem was solved and apply that solution to the current problem – using a particular kind of transaction mechanism you might have seen in the past, for example. Also, when clients understand that you have been there and seen that before, it makes them more willing to listen and try alternatives to get things done. This will separate you from a different banker who might have less experience or may be simply going by the numbers, as opposed to trying to solve a particular problem in that given transaction.

To be successful, you must try to be honest with your clients. It is no secret that bankers are biased to do transactions because of the financial reward they receive. Nevertheless, bankers who have been the most successful are those who can give clients good advice and tell them this is a transaction they should do or not do in some particular way, or it is better left for next year or some other time. The ultimate in value for a banker is advising clients not to do something and in effect becoming the client's good counselor and good advisor. In the long run, the banker may provide greater value by advising his or her client not to do something.

The measure of success is defined by your impact on clients – being able to look back at situations and identify where you made substantial contributions or brought a transaction together when it looked as though it wouldn't work. Being able to look back over time and say you made a difference in this or that situation is the primary notion of success.

The number one rule in investment baking is to listen to your client. Another is to try your best to act in your client's best interest. And don't lose the forest for the trees: Investment banking sometimes tends to be a tree-oriented business.

Gerald Rosenfeld is chief executive officer of Rothschild North America. Before joining Rothschild, he was president of G Rosenfeld & Co LLC, an investment banking firm. Prior to founding GR Co in 1998, he was head of Investment Banking and a member of the Management Committee of Lazard Freres & Co LLC. Mr. Rosenfeld joined Lazard in 1992 after holding significant management positions at Bankers Trust Company, Salomon Inc. and its Salomon Brothers subsidiary, and McKinsey & Company.

Mr. Rosenfeld joined McKinsey in 1976 and was an active member of that firm's finance practice. He joined Salomon Brothers in 1979 in the mergers and acquisitions department and was a managing director there until being named executive vice president and chief financial officer of Salomon Inc. and chief financial officer of Solomon Brothers in 1987. Mr. Rosenfeld joined Bankers Trust in 1988 as a managing director and head of the Merchant Banking Group.

Mr. Rosenfeld has worked extensively in the industrial and technology sectors, including representation of General Motors, Chrysler, United Technologies, ITT Corporation, Tenneco, TRW, Lucas Varity PLC, and Case Corporation. He has also advised on several of the largest technology mergers, including IBM's acquisition of Lotus Corp. He has served as both buy-side and strategic advisor to these and other industrial companies.

Before he joined McKinsey, Mr. Rosenfeld was a member of the faculty of the City College of New York, New York University, and the University of Maryland.

Mr. Rosenfeld is a member of the Board of Directors of Resources Connection, ContiGroup Companies, and the Jewish Theological Seminary. He also serves on the Board *of Overseers of New York University's Stern School of Business. He holds a Ph.D. in applied mathematics from New York University and is an adjunct professor of finance at the New York University Stern School of Business.*

THE ART OF BALANCING

EDUARDO G. MESTRE

Salomon Smith Barney

Vice Chairman

Investment Banking Division Chairman

Learning the Balancing Act

Much has been written about investment bankers – especially about how much money they used to make – but very little about what they actually do besides trying to collect big fees. Presumably, there must be some value in their arcane craft; otherwise, why would anybody be willing to pay those big fees?

The technical part of investment banking is not complex, but it is taxing and does require a great deal more art and a great deal more iteration than meets the eye if you aspire to create something that is actually useful. Engineers with advanced degrees in origami and oratory would probably make exceptional investment bankers, but they are hard to come by. A stint at a real job in some nice, big industrial enterprise would also probably be helpful, especially if you intend to become a so-called industry specialist. Believe it or not, it actually helps to have at least a notional understanding of the business you are trying to finance, buy, sell, or restructure.

Investment banking is first and foremost a balancing act. It requires deconstructing financial, strategic, organizational, and personal considerations into an overall cohesive package. You must give the client the best of your personal and institutional thinking, while providing the client with real choices. Although the banker may have some good ideas, sometimes there is no single right answer to a given situation, so the client needs a few viable alternatives. You have to pull a variety of things together and create several legitimate options.

Personal and institutional thinking must be combined in this balancing act. Institutions, at the end of the day, are the sum of the many different people who contribute to the resolution of what are frequently fairly complex problems. Given the number of specialists often involved in a financing or an advisory assignment, there may be several opinions, all of them credible and often all of them right. This is where you need to add your own particular perspective. The client wants more than just the opinion of the institution. Good bankers will tell the client what they think about a situation. They may have to say, "This is what I think, and here is why."

Another important component of the balancing act concerns the personal aspects of the banker's job. The way I've organized my practice, for example, reflects what I consider to be important. I find that trying to help teams is often at the top of my list. Much, if not all, of what we do necessitates working in teams because the issues we deal with are so complex. Ensuring the team develops a healthy thought process leads to good decision-making. The second thing I find important is helping people think through career issues. An individual may be thinking about going abroad, changing industry focus, or joining a product group. When considering these issues, my advice must balance what might be best for them with what might be best for the institution. The third thing I find important is trying to deliver disinterested advice. What I have to say may not be what the client wants to hear, so I must make sure the way I present information does not offend anyone. How to do this effectively is something I have learned over the course of my career.

Giving disinterested advice requires discipline and confidence. In this industry, you get paid if something happens, and you do not get paid if nothing happens. This potential conflict is inherent in the business. Clients need to understand that a young, inexperienced banker may be tempted to push for a certain deal as a way to make his mark or to generate compensation dollars. However, when you reach a certain level in an organization or stature among your peers, you find your success does not depend on what deals you do. Instead, you're more concerned about your reputation and your relationships with clients. You must make good on the trust you have gained over time. Delivering on this trust is the hallmark of a good banker.

The investment banking industry is very challenging in many other ways, as well. These challenges fall into three categories. First, this is a service industry, so you are always on call. You must always think of the client's needs first and put them above any of your own priorities. Over time, this can put a great deal of stress on your personal life. The second challenge stems from the highly competitive nature of this industry. Currently there are at least eight well-established competitors, making it difficult to succeed without always giving it your very best. The margin between success and failure is generally infinitesimal – you always win or lose by an inch. The third challenge is giving strategic advice that is thoughtful, informed, and practical. As already noted, each situation must be carefully evaluated on the facts of the particular case.

I wouldn't be in this business, though, if I didn't think the rewards outweighed the challenges. The most exciting part of my job is becoming intimately involved in what is frequently a critical decision for a company. It's extremely gratifying to be able to deliver value-added counsel in connection with that decision. And for sheer excitement, there is nothing like reading about a deal you have been working on for months on the cover of *The Wall Street Journal* or *The New York Times*. The ultimate is to make the front-page right-hand column of the *Times,* which I have experienced only twice in my career.

Key Issues in M&A and Capital-Raising Transactions

Mergers and acquisitions – one of the main areas of focus by investment bankers – present a wide range of problems and issues. Every proposed transaction is different, so it's tempting but risky to follow a textbook approach. You must be flexible and able to adjust to any and every situation. Developing a sense of what is important and what is not is also critical. You must retain maximum flexibility and adopt a willingness to adjust your strategy as facts change. You have to be a good reader of what is driving the other side – to have a sense of what will work and what won't work for them. You have to develop the skill of accurately reading people, sometimes known as emotional intelligence, or the capacity to see and feel from the other person's perspective. And you must be a good communicator, both of facts and arguments, which, in turn, must be reasonable, sound, and supportable.

Mergers are especially challenging because you have to identify the key issues that will drive a transaction, such as governance, structure, and timing. Managing expectations is also quite important. That takes a lot of preparation, as well as a willingness to deliver bad news *early.*

M&A deals become even more challenging in a turbulent economy because it is generally more difficult to have confidence about expected financial performance. Uncertainty leads to a diminished willingness to take risk, even if the opportunity is arguably compelling. Sellers will try to convince buyers that valuation must be based on normalized, not current, operating results, while buyers will be focused on worst-case scenarios. Finding common ground under these circumstances is no mean feat.

Valuing a company is a skill that improves with experience. The techniques are generally well understood, such as precedent transactions, discounted cash flow, and comparables analysis. But to apply these blindly is not always wise. Take the dot-com craze. Much of what was done was justified in terms of what others were doing. Surely one could take comfort from so many respected people singing from the same hymnal. Everybody seemed to have forgotten about railroad stock and Dutch tulips.

A combination of two companies must be predicated on the ability to produce significant synergies, which in turn must be valued. Relative value is also important in the valuation process, and this goes beyond just what the company is currently worth on the market. You must look at *all* factors. People have gotten into the habit of looking at future performance at the cost of ignoring past performance, which always has material predictive value.

When it comes to raising capital, it pays to remember that every case is different, just as every M&A situation is different. How and what type of capital is raised should be highly customized to the particular need at that time.

An initial public offering is the most prominent of the various equity financing options. The standards for determining when a company is ready for an IPO are continuously changing. In the boom of the late 1990s, all a company needed was a name, a CEO, and the outline of a business plan, but now the market has gone back to basics. Financial performance that can withstand quarterly scrutiny is necessary for a public listing. The investor deserves an established record of setting and meeting operating and financial goals before being asked to risk investment funds. There must be enough success in the past to create a sense of confidence in the future.

When assessing whether or not a company is ready for IPO, it is also important to examine the company's management team. This must be done carefully. You are judging people, so it is as much art as science. The most effective way to measure a management team is to examine its track record. This may not tell you everything you need to know – the ups and downs may have been affected more by exogenous factors than management activities – but you must make the judgment anyway. Clearly, a team that has demonstrated its ability to run a company with good margins and high growth rates is the best foundation on which to make such a judgment. Look at the track record, and benchmark it against those of other companies. When you meet the management team, you must also rely on your own instincts. You must gauge how much confidence they will inspire among employees, customers and shareholders.

Measuring Success

In selling yourself to your customers, it is wise to remember that clients can be fooled occasionally, but not frequently. The quality of your ideas and advice must be your main selling point. The client must also like and trust you. Focus on quality and integrity, and success will follow.

Always tell the client what you actually think. Internalize what you're planning to present, and present it only if it makes sense to you. Develop your own views and resist the temptation to follow someone else's lead. Don't worry about what a client *wants* to hear – you must try to tell them what they *need* to hear. This is such a competitive business that people are often reluctant to say what they should, for fear of losing business. Be true to the situation and to yourself.

The best indicator of your success as an investment banker is whether or not you have repeat clients. If clients come back to you, you know you have succeeded. That is the most telling component of success. Other metrics, such as market share, profits, and revenues are, of course, important and relevant. But repeat business is the ultimate test.

Eduardo G. Mestre is a vice chairman of Salomon Smith Barney, chairman of its Investment Banking Division, and the firm's most senior investment banker. He is also a member of the Planning Group of Citigroup's Corporate and Investment Bank, which sets policy for Citigroup's combined corporate and investment banking activities, and is a member of both its North American and European Customer Committees, which have oversight for the firm's most important client relationships. Before becoming chairman of the Investment Bank, Mr. Mestre was head of investment banking at Salomon Smith Barney and its predecessor firms for six years and co-head of Salomon Brothers' mergers and acquisitions department for six years. During his 25-year tenure at the firm, he also founded and was head of its Telecommunications Group. Prior to joining Salomon Brothers in 1977, he was an associate with the law firm of Cleary, Gottlieb, Steen & Hamilton.

Over the years Mr. Mestre has represented many clients in the communications, technology, aerospace, defense, media, and power industries. These clients have included AOL in its merger with Time Warner; Citigroup in its acquisition of Banamex, Mexico's largest bank; Worldcom in its merger with MCI; SBC in its acquisition of Ameritech; PacTel in its sale to SBC; and Northrop Grumman in its mergers with Litton and Grumman.

Mr. Mestre serves as chairman of the board of WNYC, New York's public radio stations.

Born in Havana, Cuba, in 1949, Mr. Mestre graduated summa cum laude and Phi Beta Kappa from Yale University in 1970 with a BA degree in economics and political science and is a 1973 cum laude graduate of Harvard Law School.

Other Books for Investment Banking Professionals

▸**The Investment Banking Legal Handbook** - Industry Insiders on the Laws and Documents that Govern Investment Banking Deals, Raising Capital, M&A and More - Includes Every Major Document Used With Analysis & Negotiation Points - 820 Pages - $299.95

▸**The International M&A Handbook** - A Country by Country Look at Doing Deals, Valuations, Legal Documents & More (Available August 2004-Preorder and Save $60) - $299.95

▸**Deal Teams** - Roles and Motivations of Management Team Members, Venture Capitalists, Investment Bankers, Lawyers & More in Mergers, Acquisitions and Equity Investments - $27.95

▸**Term Sheets & Valuations** - Best Selling Venture Capital Book of 2003 - Line by Line Descriptions of Each Clause and Negotiation Points - $14.95

▸**Deal Terms** - The Finer Points of Venture Capital Deal Structures, Valuations, Stock Options and Getting Deals Done - $49.95

▸**Leading Deal Makers** - Top Lawyers & VCs on Negotiations & Deal Making - $27.95

▸**Private Placement Memorandums Line by Line** - Leading Lawyer Gregory Nowak on How to Understand, Develop & Fine Tune Private Placement Memorandums - Includes Detailed Analysis of Actual Memorandum - $99.95

▸**The Art of the IPO** - Investor Relations Professionals and Leading Lawyers on IPO Strategies & Mechancis - $129.95

Buy All 8 Titles Above - Save 40%

$599.95 – Call 1-866-Aspatore (277-2867) – Phone Order Rate Only

Inside The Minds:
Leading Investment Bankers

Dedications & Acknowledgements

Daniel H. Bayly
"To all the employees of Merrill Lynch who showed remarkable dedication and courage in the face of the tragic events at the World Trade Center on September 11, 2001."

Jimmy Dunne, III
"This chapter is dedicated to the memory of Chris Quackenbush."